Journey Through History

The Contemporary Age

Translation: Jean Grasso Fitzpatrick

English translation © Copyright 1988 by Barron's Educational Series, Inc.

© Parramón Ediciones, S.A.
First Edition, February 1988
The title of the Spanish edition is *La edad contemporánea*

All inquiries should be addressed to:
Barron's Educational Series, Inc.
250 Wireless Boulevard
Hauppauge, New York 11788

Library of Congress Catalog Card No. 88-10390
International Standard Book No. 0-8120-3394-9
Library of Congress Cataloging-in-Publication Data

Vergés, Gloria.
  [Edad contemporánea. English]
  The Contemporary age / [illustrated by] Carme Peris; [written by]
Gloria & Oriol Vergés; [translation, Jean Grasso Fitzpatrick]. —
1st ed.
    p. cm. — (Journey through history)
  Translation of: Edad contemporánea.
  Summary: An introductory history of the nineteenth and twentieth
centuries, with a fictional story involving children to depict the era.
  ISBN 0-8120-3394-9
  1. History, Modern—19th century—Juvenile literature.
2. History, Modern—20th century—Juvenile literature.
[1. History, Modern—19th century. 2. History, Modern—20th
century.] I. Peris, Carme, ill. II. Vergés, Oriol. III. Title.
IV. Series: Vergés, Gloria. Viaje a través de la historia.
English.
D358.V4813 1988
909.8—dc19   88-10390
                                              CIP
Printed in Spain by Sirven Grafic   AC
Gran Vía, 754 Barcelona
Legal Deposit: B-19.612-88

890   987654321

Journey Through History

The Contemporary Age

Carme Peris
Glòria & Oriol Vergés

New York · Toronto · Sydney

In our great-grandparents' day, democracy already existed in some European countries and in the United States. Citizens could elect the people they wanted to represent them in government. People got used to the election process, but not everyone could vote as we do today. In some countries poor people did not have the right to vote, and women could not vote anywhere.

"My mother is very angry because she is not allowed to vote."

"Mine too, but she says soon women will have the same legal rights as men."

Until the early twentieth century, England, France, and other European countries had colonies—territories outside of Europe that were ruled from the mother country.

The European countries took farm products and minerals from their colonies and carried them back home, where they were refined in factories or traded.

On occasion, the colonial governors allowed their officials to treat the natives cruelly. However, the missionaries, doctors, and teachers did a great deal of good.

"Look, they've cured your brother! The white doctors know more than our witch doctors."

"How wonderful! But now I'm afraid that he will be sent back to the fields to pick coffee beans."

As new factories were built, there was more conflict between owners and workers. The workers wanted a shorter work week and higher wages.

Sometimes, the only way the workers felt they could make themselves heard was by going on strike. They would stop working until they either ran out of money or got what they demanded. Soon, labor unions were created which fought for better wages and working conditions. A theory called *socialism* was developed. It proposed changes in society so that there would no longer be such great differences between one group of people and another.

With the improvement of the microscope, *microbiology*—the science that studies the germs that cause illness—made great progress.

Now medicine succeeded in preventing and curing many deadly diseases and halting their spread. Children and adults were immunized, and the great epidemics disappeared in the more advanced countries. Furthermore, diseases that had been considered incurable were wiped out. Fewer children died, and adults lived longer.

"Do you know what I'm doing when I immunize you? I'm injecting you with a small amount of the weakened germ that produces the infection. This will cause your body to develop an immunity to the germ. That way you'll probably never catch the disease itself."

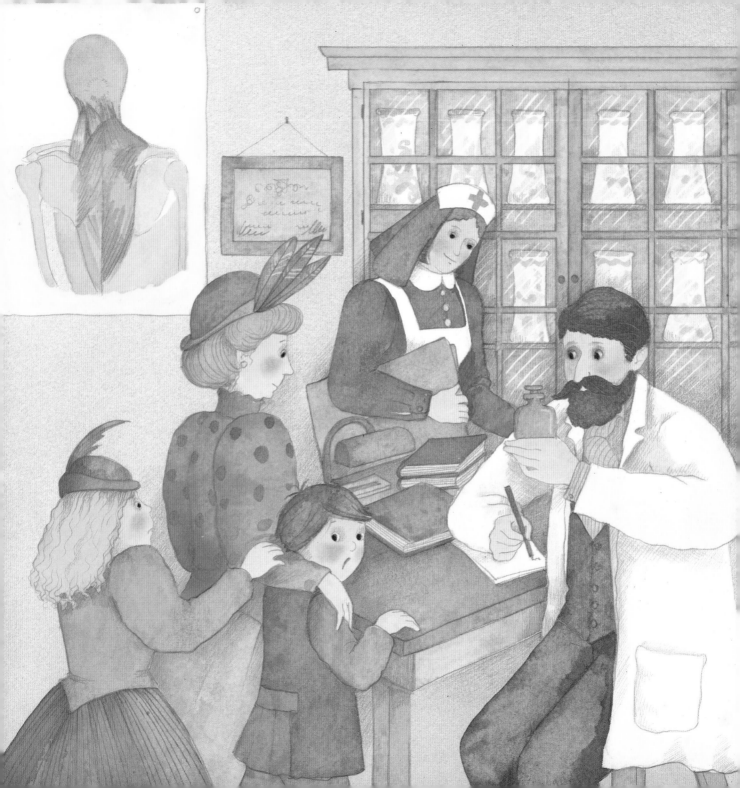

The automobile represented a huge improvement in transporting goods and people. Highways were built alongside the old roads which had been constructed during Roman times. Where the railways hadn't arrived—in highly mountainous areas or far away places—cars could, and did travel, followed by buses and trucks.

At first, people living in the countryside were frightened by the automobile's speed and the sound of its horn.

"I'm not afraid of them anymore. I'm used to these machines!"

"Maybe you are, but the chickens certainly aren't! My father is very angry because last week two of them were run over!"

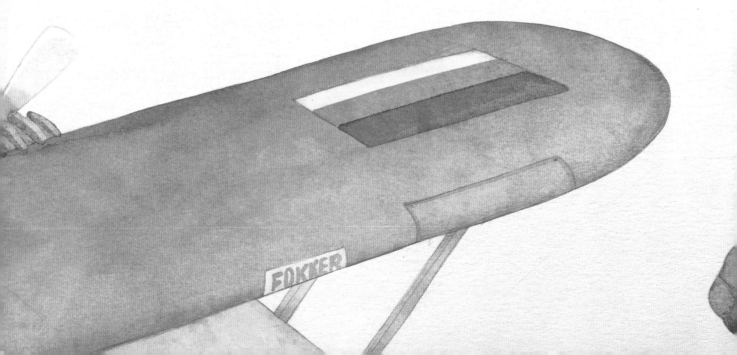

The last great victory for transportation was the airplane. With it, the old dream of flying really had come true. Now passengers felt safe, and the pilot could actually decide in which direction to fly.

In time, the airlines opened routes to the distant corners of each country and, indeed, the world. It was a great advance in transportation, but also an opportunity to improve communication between all nations.

"I don't think you or I will ever end up flying in one of these things."

"In a few years we surely will. My teacher says that engineers will build airplanes so big that they will be able to carry many passengers. Then I will fly all over the world."

Moving pictures—that is, films or movies—continued what the theater had done in the past. Movies allow audiences to relive the past or imagine themselves as the main characters having exciting adventures. People's need to escape from everyday problems helped the rapid growth of the movie industry.

The first silent films were performed by actors who constantly made faces and gestures so the audience could understand the plot. Every so often, printed words on screen also helped explain the action.

"Latest news! Hot off the presses!"

Life in the cities underwent many changes during the twentieth century. Newspapers, which had existed since the previous century, and radio, which was a great novelty, kept people informed about events of the world.

News reached the most isolated areas. Later, it would be television that would bring viewers "on location" with the news.

Besides new inventions, other developments changed people's lives. For instance, women began to gain power and to participate in politics for the first time.

Despite all this progress, the world was not at peace. Two world wars destroyed fields and cities and brought death and misery to millions of innocent families. Scientific advances were used to make war, and much more powerful weapons began to be manufactured. During World War I, many European towns and cities were bombed. During the Second World War, all the continents became battlefields. Up to this point no one had imagined how much destruction bombs could bring.

To avoid disasters like the world wars, the United Nations (UN) organization was created. The UN is an assembly where countries discuss their differences and sign agreements that solve some of their problems.

Unfortunately, the UN has not been able to prevent war or the control of powerful countries over weaker ones. The UN also has a series of organizations which are designed to promote peace and well-being in the world. The FAO helps solve the problem of hunger in developing countries. UNICEF works with children in the poorest countries to help them become healthy and educated. As these children grow up, they will be able to help improve life in their countries.

Sports have become very important in our century. There are increasing numbers of athletes and millions of fans who follow the games of their favorite teams.

To promote peace and friendship among all the nations of the world, the modern Olympics are celebrated. The top athletes from every country compete. These contests also help show off the host country and its customs to all those who travel there for the Olympic Games.

"It's exciting to think that competitions like this were once celebrated in ancient Greece."

"Yes, but now they bring together men and women from all over the world—not just from one country as they did then."

The richest countries in the world are now involved in what is known as the "space race." That means they are competing to make the advances needed, not only to travel through space, but also to set up artificial satellites and space stations where people can someday live.

Without a doubt, the most spectacular moment of this space race was the landing of people on the moon. Now the old dream of flying reached heights that up until then only science fiction writers had been able to imagine. Spectators from all over the world excitedly watched on television as a man took his first steps on the moon's surface.

Of course, these advances should serve to promote peace. The results of using nuclear power and artificial satellites for war could be terrible.

Science is constantly changing our leisure activities and our work lives.

We must hope that this road, along which we are moving so rapidly, will lead to the progress and well-being of all people.

"My father told me that he will give me a new computer that's even more powerful than my old one."

"I don't want to change mine yet. I still don't know how to do everything with the one I have now."

The child should understand that, beginning with the Industrial Revolution, technological advances took place with extraordinary speed. In an endless spiral, each discovery generates new technological inventions which, in turn, lead to new discoveries.

European Colonialism

Colonialism was highly profitable for many countries. The mother countries obtained the raw materials they needed from their colonies, and then processed them. Often they disguised their economic interest by claiming that their goal was to bring culture to the natives, but the culture they brought was obviously foreign.

The Growing Population

The drop in infant mortality rate and the increase in lifespan due to medical advances have brought to the world the problem of overpopulation. In the developing countries, above all, sociologists say that it is obvious that rapid population growth is a direct cause of mass poverty.

The Labor Movement

At first, the workers were subject to the interests of the factory owners. Then the struggle for freedom became recognized by those in power. In many nations technology has improved the way of life for both the workers and owners.

The Transportation Revolution

Advances in transportation have made the world smaller, not only in terms of travel but also in the communication of ideas. Today, no one should be ignorant of the events—tragic or happy—of the world.

Feeding the World's Population

The FAO, the Food and Agriculture Organization of the United Nations, is dedicated to helping developing countries feed themselves. New technology has increased food production, but the chemicals in certain pesticides and fertilizers have caused serious health problems.

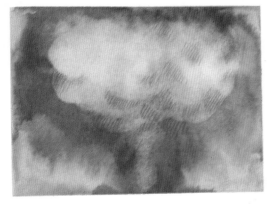

The Danger of War

World wars should never be repeated. The causes were economic and territorial interests, in the case of World War I, and the rise of fascism in World War II. The terrible consequences—millions of deaths, territorial divisions, and hate and enmity between people—have not been forgotten.

The Importance of Peace

The great powers keep increasing and improving their arsenals, even while negotiation disarmament agreements for certain classes of weapons. The arms race is a dangerous one that could end up destroying humanity. Children should understand clearly that attaining peace is the highest ideal people should pursue. They should learn to reject violence and to communicate in good will.

Technology and Human Need

Information systems are changing the world of work and some of our most deep-rooted traditions. Children should learn about technology, but they need to understand that computers are machines that can be useful but must always be at the service of our collective well-being.